199 Power Prayers for the New Year

Pamela McQuade

BARBOUR
PUBLISHING

Published by Barbour Publishing, Inc., P.O. Box 719, Uhrichsville, Ohio 44683, www.barbourbooks.com

Our mission is to publish and distribute inspirational products offering exceptional value and biblical encouragement to the masses.

 Member of the
Evangelical Christian
Publishers Association

Printed in the United States of America.

Introduction

The start of a New Year offers us the opportunity to consider where we've been in life and to evaluate our spiritual direction. As the New Year begins, we need to spend time in prayer—setting God-given goals for the next 365 days. Our first priority may be making a resolution to spend time with God, reading His Word, and speaking intimately with Him. He cares about our days and the joys and struggles that fill them, but if we are always too busy for quiet time with Him, His Spirit is unlikely to deeply touch our hearts.

Though we may not call them resolutions, every year we all make plans and identify elements of our lives that we need to change. The topics covered in this collection of prayers are some major areas of concern in our lives—places in which we need to draw ever nearer to God. Improvements in these areas can develop our relationship with the Savior. All year long, we can make use of the prayers in this volume to develop our lives.

Use these prayers as inspiration for your personal prayers, a starting place for seeking out God's perfect will for your life. With daily, intimate, consistent communion with Him, we all can draw nearer to Jesus.

CONTENTS

My Relationships. 7

My Work. 16

My Health. 26

My Spiritual Life. 36

My Church 46

My Future 55

My Finances 64

My Praise 72

My Friends 80

My Family. 88

MY RELATIONSHIPS

The most important relationship
I have is the one with You, my God.
May our connection always inform and
guide my attitudes and actions with
other people. I want You to be
at the center of my life.

Lord, relationships can be so wonderful—
and so hard. Too often sin interrupts
my peace and makes things more difficult
than I'd like. In this New Year, pour out
Your Spirit on my relationships
so they glorify You.

Sometimes I need to start over in
relationships, Lord. May this change in
year be time to get on course with those
I love. I resolve to seek forgiveness where
I need to and build bridges of hope in all
my relationships. Thank You, Lord, for
the blessing of having friends, family, and
fellow Christians to relate to. Help me
appreciate each person who touches my life
over the next several months; may I also
be a blessing to them.

Love is patient and kind,
but sometimes I find it hard to express.
Jesus, this year fill my mouth with gentle
words and my life with good actions
that show what it means to
love others through You.

Help me see honestly, Jesus,
if I love anyone more than I love You. If so,
I need to confess that sin and make a
change. Then spark my devotion to You
and make me realize how much I need You.
In these months, be first in my heart.

You've told me to love others, Jesus.
Whether I find that difficult or easy in
the next year, may I be a light to those
who live near me. Show me how to reach
out and touch anyone I meet in my
community, however briefly.

Lord, I dedicate myself anew to putting Your truths into action during the next twelve months. Make my life a consistent service for You. Work through me to bring Your grace to others.

I need to have a good working relationship with my boss, Lord Jesus. Together, help us erase any kinks that may wind their way into our lives. I want to serve You and my company well.

What can be more important in this year
than communing with You, O Lord?
Out of this communion develop
all other relationships. Help me to
consistently come to You in prayer.

Romance can be such an invigorating
experience, Lord. Thank You for creating it.
But I know You have a higher purpose
for it, too. Help my romantic
life to serve You always.

I have fleeting relationships with
many people, Lord Jesus. But even in
an instant, I give others an opinion of
me—and You, too. This year, may my
every action consistently glorify You so
that all may come to love You.

Without close relationships, I become
lonely, Lord. Sometimes others seem far
away, though I know they care for me.
That's when I need to draw near to You
in a special way. Remind me this year
that You are my best Friend of all,
my Father, and my elder Brother.

Provide me, Lord, with at least one
challenging friendship that makes me
grow in You. I want to relate to someone
who's profoundly committed to You
and encourages me to reach my
potential in commitment, too.

Lord, You told us to love our neighbors,
knowing how hard that can be. This year
I plan to appreciate the folks who live
close by me, even if I don't always
understand them or agree with them.
Give me grace to accomplish that goal.

Help me see how I treat the children in my
life, Jesus. Remind me that You drew them
to Yourself in love, and I need to love them
gently, too. This year I want to treat
youngsters with Your respect.

Sometimes I feel the impact of a generation gap, when I talk to those younger or older than me. Remind me that either I once was their age or I hope to live as long as they have. May I patiently listen to them and understand their hearts and minds.

In any year, some people whom I love deeply will exit from my life, and I will feel the pain of losing a close relationship. Help me, Lord, to bring truths I learned from that love into new relationships.

When I come to the end of this year, I want to have grown in Your love, Lord. Help me carry all I've learned from You and the relationships that have stretched me into another New Year. Help me share what I've learned with others, too.

MY WORK

Whether I work at home or
in a large office, You have designed a plan
for my life. Thank You, Lord, for providing
for me. Help me serve You consistently
as I work for and with others.

I know, Lord, my work life shouldn't be
separate from my faith. This year, help me
to be consistent for You. May all I do be of
benefit to both You and the place where I
work. Aid me also to bless my coworkers
as I connect with them in love.

It's a beautiful day, Lord, and I'd rather
be having fun than working. Give me a new
resolution to ignore the distractions and
show others what it means to faithfully
serve You in the workplace.

In any job there's always one
person who's hard to work with,
Lord. This year, help me love even
my most difficult coworker.

Am I too comfortable in my job, Lord?
Is it time for me to seek something new
that will stretch my talents? Help me move
beyond my comfortable station and grow
in ability and strength. But no matter
where I go, give me a ministry for You.

Deadlines overwhelm me, Lord,
but they don't overwhelm You.
Help me find a way to make this one—
even though it seems impossible.

Some days I enjoy my job, but on others
I'd rather not be working. Help me serve
clients—and especially You—no matter
what the state of my emotions.

I know I need to balance my work, home,
and spiritual lives, Lord. This year give
me wisdom so I can understand
what's important to Your kingdom.
I need to use my time wisely.

My coworkers face many challenges,
both on the job and at home. As I pray,
keep me mindful of their needs—especially
those who have never known Your love.

You've given me work to engage mind
and body, Lord. Help me bring my spirit
to it, too. I want my whole being
working together for You.

When I look back at the beginning of
my career, Lord God, I'm amazed at how
far You've brought me. Thank You
for Your blessings each year.

Give me a vision, Lord, of the direction
I should take this year in my work life.
Show me ways to serve others and
improve my career. I always want
to walk in Your path.

What happens at work doesn't always
please You, Lord, and that doesn't please
me. But together we can change lives.
Let's do it!

All I do should serve You, Lord Jesus.
Keep me patient with clients, supportive
of coworkers, and honest in all things.
Help my career reflect Your love every day,
in as many ways as possible.

Some days work seems as if it's my whole world, Lord, as I get caught up in what I need to do. Remind me that being a child of God is more important than how I make a living. Let me truly live for You.

I have days that seem like drudgery, Lord, and others in which the time flies by as I accomplish a lot. Both are just part of my working experience. No matter how many of each I experience this year, may I have success in serving You on the job.

At some point, we all have a job we don't like, Lord. If I fall into that trap this year, help me find something new in which I can serve You with all my heart. I don't want to work in the wrong place.

Not only do I work in a career, Lord, I need to work on some things at home and church that get put aside when my career becomes demanding. Help me find time for those things that really need doing around the house and in service to You, too.

When my work cannot glorify You, Lord,
it's time for a new career or position. Help
me find something new that will help
me serve You better. Bring me into good
relationships on a new job and let me
perform some worthwhile service, too.

I need to pray for the company I work for,
Lord. May it not only be successful but
compassionate, too. May it be the kind
of company Christians can serve You in.
For the next twelve months, keep me
faithful in prayer for all its leaders.

My Work

MY HEALTH

Lord, it's a beautiful day,
and I'm glad to be out exercising. Thank
You for giving me health and strength.
May this be a year in which I stay in good
shape so I can effectively execute
Your will in my life.

You've given us a world filled with
many good foods, Father God. But there's
a lot available that's not so good, too. Help
me choose well what I put in my mouth
so I can eat wisely and stay healthy.

When I'm not feeling well, it's
hard to look ahead with confidence, Lord.
Help me to trust that every part of my
body is Yours. Nothing can happen to
me that You cannot heal or help.

Lord, I need to do many things to
improve my health or keep myself in top
shape. Guide me in making these part of
my everyday living plan. I want to have
many days on this earth, working for You.

O Lord, I am "fearfully and wonderfully made." My body does amazing things, because You've designed it so effectively. Thank You, Lord, for this gift You've given me.

There are things I can change about my health and those I can't, Lord. Sometimes my genes will lead me in places I'd rather not go, into health problems I never imagined. In those times, remind me that You are anywhere I am.

My whole being is interconnected.
Body, mind, and spirit either work together
or are damaged by one another. This year,
may my spirit so influence mind and body
that Your peace rules throughout me.

Father God, You've given me health
as a blessing. May I use it each
day to bring joy to others.

Just as I feed my soul with Your Word,
Lord God, I need to feed my body with
good things. Sometimes I eat more calories
than I need. If my eating is unhealthy,
show me where I need to make changes.
Even in this, I can glorify You.

I want to be healthy, Lord, but I don't want
to put so much emphasis on my body that
I miss out on the best You have for me.
This year, keep my body, mind,
and spirit in balance, so I never emphasize
one at a great cost to another.

Today I feel on top of the world,
Lord, because my body's in peak condition.
Thank You for that blessing.
May I use my energy well.

I know stress can be bad for me in
many ways, Lord. In the next months,
guide me to manage it wisely and use
it to accomplish more for You.

I don't want to waste my years and
energy on unimportant things, Lord.
Help me focus my physical strength on
doing the most important things for You.
Show me just what I need to do today.

Some days it's challenging to do the things I need to for health. Throughout the seasons, remind me that my body is a gift from You, Lord, and that I have a responsibility for its upkeep. I want to take good care of the body You've gifted me with, Father.

Staying healthy takes some commitment, Lord. Taking care of my body takes time and effort, whether I'm exercising or going to see a doctor for a checkup. Don't let me skimp on doing what I need to do to stay healthy this year.

Thank You, Lord, for blessing me
with good health. May I avoid taking it
for granted in the 365 days ahead.

Lord, I know You've given doctors much
knowledge and some wisdom. Guide mine
in understanding the bodies you've made
and providing me with good care.

When I feel at the bottom of the world
because my health is less than perfect,
I need You to lift my spirits, Lord.
Help to focus on Your faithfulness and to
feel the touch of Your healing Spirit.
Keep me from doubt and fear.

When my physical health is less than
wonderful, my spiritual health often gets
into trouble, too, Lord. Keep me healthy
in both ways, Lord Jesus—I need
to depend completely on You.

Lord, this year I need to make some
changes in my life to better my health.
Help me choose wisely the paths I
should take to health. I don't want to
be fooled by fads. I want to live in a
sensibly healthy way for You.

MY SPIRITUAL LIFE

As the New Year starts,
it's time to take account of my spiritual
existence, Lord. I want to take stock,
improve myself, and appreciate all You've
done for me. Give me a clear vision
of change and a sense of direction
through the next months.

Your Word, O Lord, is a real key
to my spiritual life. Help me be consistent
in reading and studying it. May my
life also reflect the truths I learn as
I put them into practice each day.
I want to be faithful to You.

Where do You want me to go
this year, Lord? Put my feet on the right
path at church, in the home, and at work.
Then enable me to walk consistently on it!

Keep me faithful in prayer throughout
these months, Lord Jesus. When I
don't pray, I don't communicate with You,
and I don't know how I should live. I want
to be close to You all 365 days of this year.
Only then can I do all Your will.

Make mine a servant's heart, Lord.
May I constantly seek to serve others
and draw them to You. Then my
New Year will be profitable.

As I begin this year, Lord, help me develop
spiritual plans. I commit myself now to
following the Christian disciplines that
help build a strong faith. Make this
a profitable year for my spirit.

Lord, I want this to be a year of persistent, powerful prayer. Draw me into Your presence and open my heart to Your will.

Draw me near to You, O Lord. My time on earth loses its value if I'm not in communion with You.

Thank You, Jesus, for calling me to Your side in salvation. Where would I be without You? I want to appreciate Your saving grace each day this year.

Your Spirit never leaves me, Lord, no
matter what challenge I face. The future is
no surprise to You, and Your Spirit cannot
lead me astray. I can always trust You to
direct my life in the best path. Thank You,
Jesus, for Your guidance this year.

Every year I face some discouragements,
Lord. May those I face this year make
me more faithful, drawing me
ever closer to Your side.

I want to live passionately for You, Jesus.
Through the next months may
my life show what it means to be
committed to You, heart and soul.

Lord, You know it's good for me to
consider my spiritual growth. Today help
me consider my ways, evaluate each,
and decide how I need to reset my
course toward You. Improve my
spiritual walk this year.

When all the spheres of my life pull me in
different directions, I need to spend time
with You most of all, Jesus. As I pray,
help me understand how You want
me to live and how to organize
my life around Your will.

Living well for You, Lord,
isn't something I do in a single day.
Help me make a year-long commitment
to growth and service. I don't want
this to be an ordinary year, and it
doesn't have to be, in You.

I know some people who have real health
problems, Jesus. Help me support them
in their pain, through prayer and action.
May they find real health in You.

It's easy to become spiritually proud,
Lord, when my life runs smoothly. Please
remind me that when life seems easy, it's
because of Your blessing, not because I'm a
super Christian. As the seasons change,
keep me mindful of my own weakness.

Life can be very frustrating, Lord, and I
may feel tempted to react harshly. I need
Your grace to remain relaxed and patient.
This year, keep my mind and heart
on You, not on my frustrations.
I want to treat others well.

Some days I'm on top of the world
spiritually, Lord. I feel so close to You and
know You are near. Remind me that our
deep relationship is not designed
just to make me feel good—I need to
share Your love with others, too.

Every moment of every day,
I need to be aware of Your love and
seek to live in Your will. Continually
fill me with Your blessed Spirit every
day of this year, so I can walk
in You each moment.

MY CHURCH

You gave me my church, Lord, as a place in which to worship You. Please give my church leaders the wisdom and knowledge to serve You well. Help me support them as they work to make this a year of great spiritual growth.

Together, help my church and me to seek Your will every day. We want to complete all the good things You have planned for us in the next months. May we constantly seek Your wisdom in everything.

My Church

I love church, Lord, but it can
also be a challenge. Guide me in
love for others this year.

Lord, You've made my church a community
of loving hearts. In the next four seasons,
our congregants will experience all
the seasons of the soul. Help us minister
well to each other, whatever the needs.

Lord, bless those who teach in my church.
Give them a deep relationship with
You this year. May their words
faithfully reflect You and stir others
to love and serve You more.

My church faces some spiritual tests,
Lord. Remind me that none of them are
unknown to You. Help us to deal with
all problems together in Your love.

You've used my church, Lord,
to draw people to Yourself. May it
consistently bring glory to You,
bringing sinners to salvation and
believers to deeper faith.

Through my church, Lord, You've given me
some ministry that helps others. Guide me
in all I do. May my ministry help many
and build me up spiritually, too.

My Church

Remind me, Lord, that the church is
made up of Your people, both those who
are effective and those who fail.
Help me love and support each one.

Have I done enough for Your church, Jesus?
Or am I over-engaged in church duties at
the expense of other important parts of my
life? Help me achieve balance so I can serve
You effectively in each realm of my life.

My church supports other ministries,
from parachurch groups to overseas
missionaries. Remind me to pray
for each of them and support them
through my finances and actions.

My church has a mission in our community
that You have set for it. As I plan to
take part in ministry, help me decide
how I can best contribute to my
church's goals this year.

Touch my pastor, Lord, with Your
Spirit's special power. Give him wisdom
and strength for the year ahead, and
through the benefits of his ministry, help
our whole church glorify You.

No spiritual community is perfect, Lord,
but many truly bless the world and draw
others to You. Help me make my church
one of them. Though we are not flawless,
help us shine brightly for You.

My Church

There are so many unsung heroes in my
church, Lord, who keep it going through
their quiet but faithful work. Help me
to support and encourage them. I want
to appreciate what they do for You
and to help them be effective.

Lord, bless the people who make up the
body of my church. Give them love and
comfort. Make this body a unified body,
strengthened by your Spirit and Your love,
gathered to meet in Your presence,
formed to do Your will.

Remind me, Lord, that there are many
faithful Christians in other churches.
Help me reach out to other believers
who are lovingly following You, whatever
congregation they belong to.

We know that through commonplace
things Satan can attack us as a church, Lord
God. Help us be wise, avoiding trouble
before it burgeons into a congregation-
wide problem. Draw us ever nearer to
You and to each other in love.

My Church

May my church not only reach out to those nearby but seek to tell the entire world about You, Jesus. Give us an increased heart for missions beyond our doorstep and wisdom concerning where and how we can best help others.

You've told us, Lord, that a physical building isn't really a church. The real church is the people who worship You. Though we need to care for our building, help our church focus on people more than things. May our love for You always come first.

Pastors can find church leadership a real stress, Lord. Remind me of that and help me treat my pastor and his family well. May our entire congregation be a blessing to a faithful leader.

MY FUTURE

When I look into the future, I see
a big blank, Lord. I don't know how
many challenges or delights I'll face.
Help me trust that whatever I confront,
You'll stand by me and bless me.

Though I'm making some big plans,
Lord, they'll all be failures if You aren't
at their center. I place my goals and ideas
for achieving them into Your hands;
this year, show me the way I
should go. May I never stray from
Your purpose for my life.

Every January 1, You remind me
of Your new life in me. I can make a new
start, Lord, with another twelve months
of living. Thank You for making me
aware of the continual refreshing
of life in Your Spirit.

Sometimes my plans for tomorrow
need fine-tuning, Jesus. I know how
easily I get distracted and wander off
Your path. If I need to turn around or
go down another road, show me.
I want to walk in Your way.

My Future

I need to look to the future, Lord.
Show me the people who can help me
choose wise goals that suit my gifts and
Your will for my life. Guide me in my
quest to accomplish Your endeavors.

Though I need to look to the future, I can't
look into it. No one but You, Lord, knows
what will happen tomorrow. Keep me from
putting my trust in anyone who tells me
otherwise. I want to trust only in You.

The life I live today is not perfect, Lord.
I need to work on many things about
myself in order to have a successful
future. Help me identify where I need to
change and resolve to more perfectly
follow Your will.

As I resolve to make life changes in the year
ahead, Lord, I know that some are likely to
fail. Help me not to rely on my willpower
for renovation but on Your power.
I want to change.

As I walk into the future, Lord, You
remind me that I don't get everything I
want right away. Give me the strength and
patience to wait for the best, instead
of requiring instant gratification.

My Future

Lord, please take command of the
365 days yet to come. You are Lord of all.
When each twenty-four-hour segment is
in Your hands, I can never fail.

No one guarantees tomorrow to me,
Father God. But each day of my life is in
Your control, and I need to be ready for all
that may happen. Help me trustingly look
into the future and prepare for it.

I have many plans and goals, Lord. I usually
pray about them as I start something new,
but sometimes I get so caught up that
I forget to make certain You are guiding
me as I carry them out. Help me to share
every step of the way with You.

Though I do my best to plan for the future,
You know, O Lord, that life often
throws me a curve. Then You remind
me the best plan for the future is Yours.
Help me make Your plans mine.

Lord Jesus, You've given me dreams for
my life. Even when they seem unlikely
to happen, help me to trustingly keep
them alive in my spirit. May I accomplish
all You want me to in life.

Every year You set wonderful opportunities
before me, Lord. I want to try new things,
meet new people, and go new places. But
help me not to do anything simply for the
excitement of doing it. Keep me
ever in Your will.

Where will I go in the next twelve months,
Lord? I cannot know, since life is ever
changing. But You never alter, Father.
Remind me of that when I begin
to doubt. My trust remains in You.

You've made it clear, Father, that in the
next months I have two choices: I can live
in You or in the world. Though the world's
way is often tempting, give me strength
to follow You alone.

I look forward to eternity with great joy,
Jesus, when I think of the good things
You have stored up for me. When life on
earth doesn't seem so cheerful, I need
Your strength. This year, help me
cling to You, in joy or stress.

A year can bring much change, Lord.
I need to be steadfast in faith and love
for You. Keep my heart ever heading
in Your direction, no matter where
I travel spiritually. Let's get to
our destination together.

Lord, Your Word shows me what you have
in store for me and everyone here on earth.
Your promises will never fail. Help me
take them seriously, in my own life and as
I touch the lives of others. I want many to
join me in heaven.

My Future

MY FINANCES

Since You spoke so often about money
during Your ministry, Lord Jesus, I know
that what I do with mine is important
to You. Help me seek Your will
concerning how I spend every paycheck.
Make my money Your money, Lord.

You have blessed me with so much, Lord,
though I often take it for granted.
This year, help me remember and
appreciate the blessings You give—
then share them with others.

My Finances

You know I'd like to give much more than
I can afford, Lord. There are so many
good causes out there. Help me to choose
wisely over the next twelve months.
And never let me forget my church,
which needs my regular support.

Money isn't ultimately important, Lord,
except in the way it shows my love
for You. This year, may I use every
penny to do Your will.

Help me purchase wisely, whether
I'm buying a house or housewares, Lord.
I want to use all my resources to
further Your kingdom.

I want to use all my money wisely. Help me to understand how it can glorify You and how I can use it for that purpose. Everything in my life, Lord, should honor You.

I can make investments in Your kingdom, Lord, and earthly investments for my future. I need to do both. Please give me Your wisdom to know when and how to invest in each. I want to be prepared for both my earthly needs and eternity.

When I invest in Your kingdom, You will never fail me, Lord Jesus. I know I can never outgive You. When You test my faith and finances, keep me strong. This year, may selfishness never become my way of life.

My Finances

I know my finances will affect my church,
too, Lord God. Help me to give all
I can to spread Your Word to others.
I don't want to shortchange You.

I need to put aside money for the future,
Jesus. Help me plan ahead and save
for the things that lie ahead, whether
it's retirement, a home, or a nest egg.
Don't let me be so caught up in today
that I fail to look before me.

Help me know the difference
between wants and needs, Lord.
You have promised You'll provide my needs.
Help me control my want list.

Thank You, Jesus, for providing for
all my needs. I am awed at Your love
for me, which extends to all the details
of my life—even my checkbook.

Everyone needs a budget, Lord,
no matter how much money's coming in.
Help me to use my money wisely and
send enough Your way.

Remind me, O Lord, of others whose need
is so much greater than mine. Help me to
be generous in spreading Your blessings
where they are most needed.

My Finances

I can learn about my finances from others
who are wise with money, Lord. Help
me find these faithful people and learn
how to best glorify You with all that I
make over the next twelve months.

Lord, You've given me gifted people who
have helped me save money when I needed
something done on my home. They helped
fix anything from a bookshelf to a major
part of my house. I appreciate them—
help me remember to give them thanks
and return the favor, if possible.

It's sometimes hard for me to tell, Lord,
if I'm loving money more than I love You.
Make me aware of any material
element that would keep me from giving
You first place in my heart. Nothing can
fill my heart the way You do.

I know from Your Word, Jesus, that people
should be more important than money.
Help me use my income to serve others
and You. I want to provide for myself
and my family, but I need to reach
out to the world, too.

It's hard, Lord, to keep a good perspective
on how much money should go to each
place in my budget. Help me balance
everything effectively so I can use all
my income wisely for Your kingdom.

Responsibility is an important part of using
money to glorify You, Lord, but it's often
uncomfortable because being responsible
means I must deny myself. Help me
remember where irresponsibility will lead me
and how blessed I am when I follow You.

My Finances

MY PRAISE

I love You, my glorious Lord,
my one and only Savior.
Knowing You has changed my
whole life, and I am so blessed!

Another year! I rejoice that I'll have 365
days in which to praise Your name.
Lord, please make this a praise-filled year,
no matter what I face. If trials come
my way, You'll never fail me. I'll still
enjoy Your blessings each day.
Let's walk into this year together.

My Praise

My heart swells with praise for You,
O Lord. Your love reaches into every corner
of my soul, and I face a bright future in
You. May Your Spirit daily fill me with
the joys of Your love. I want to
draw ever nearer to You.

Today, O Lord, I'm making a sacrifice of
praise. Though I don't feel life is very good,
I know it is, because You still love me.
Even on this year's sad days, You lift my
heart to the skies. Thank You, my Jesus.

Your grace has followed me, O Lord,
everywhere I've gone in life. As I head
into a new, uncharted year, help
me walk in Your will.

Some days I worship You easily, Lord.
Other times, worship is more duty than
fun. But keep me faithful in Your love
every day of the year. I know You love me,
even on my dark and difficult days.

In eternity, I will praise You forever, my
King. Don't let me enter heaven's gates
unprepared because I have inadequately
praised You on earth. Help me
sing about my joy in You today.

I praise You for the good things You've done
in others' lives, Lord. I've recognized Your
powerful hand at work and been thankful.
Those You've aided have influenced my
life and the lives of those I love in practical
ways, too. I praise You for it all.

How glad I am to be able to praise You,
O Lord, because I have an intimate
relationship with You. Draw me
ever nearer to Your side in love.

O glorious Redeemer, thank You for Your
compassionate love that reached out to me
when I was totally lost. Your salvation has
changed me completely. Help me share
that change with others this year.

O Jesus, may worship be an important part
of my life during the next twelve months.
At church or privately, I want to praise
You every day. Make me aware of all the
good things You have placed in my life
so I may thank You constantly.

Jesus, I'm awed at the love and compassion
You have poured into my life. I enjoy all
You do for me, day by day. Help me make
that clear to others by daily living out a
clear testimony to Your salvation.

Not everyone appreciates hearing words
of praise for You, Lord. When I hear
negative responses from a hardened heart,
help me to forgive and pray for
that endangered soul.

I don't want others to praise me, Lord;
instead, I want them to recognize
all the good things You've done in me.
May my delight in knowing You be
contagious to the rest of the world.

My Praise

The wonderful things Your people do when they faithfully respond to Your Word, bring a shout of joy to my lips. Thank You for sending these faithful Christians my way so I can come to You in love and praise.

In Your kingdom we will ever praise You, Lord. In the seasons ahead, prepare me for eternity by giving me an active praise life here on earth. I don't want to come into heaven without the joy of knowing You deeply in the here and now.

I am so glad You've given me the opportunity to praise You in this life, Lord. This year, help me recognize Your worth and grace and sing Your praises more often. I want to appreciate You and Your love for me.

When I face sorrow, remind me, Lord,
that Your steadfast love endures forever.
No matter what this earth throws at me,
I can continue in praise for You. Though
my nature changes, Yours never will.
You never fail me, glorious Lord.

Sometimes giving You praise is a challenge,
Lord, when my life seems filled with
troubles. Keep my eyes on You and Your
many blessings so I do not get lost in my
own worries and fail to give You Your due.

May my life be a praise prayer to You,
O Lord, King of the universe. I plan to
sing Your praises every day, to let the
world know of Your gracious salvation.

My Praise

MY FRIENDS

Take control of the time I spend with
my friends, Jesus. I dedicate the next 365
days to You, including the time spent with
friends. May we use those days well.
Help us to bless each other and minister
to others in Your name.

Thank You, Lord, for my friends.
They fill my heart with joy.
Let us share Your love in all we do
during the days ahead.

My friends have taught me love,
compassion, and teamwork, Lord.
Thank You for building our relationships
in Your love. May our eyes always
be focused on You.

Lord, if I move or change jobs this year,
help me keep in touch with old friends
while I make new ones. I don't want to
forget people from my past, but I need to
live in the present and future, too.

In any year, Lord, I gain new friends and
lose old ones. Life is always changing.
Help me choose friends wisely and never
lose touch with the ones who bring Your
blessings and share my spiritual goals.

Help me remember, Lord, that to be a good
friend, I need to give, not simply receive.
Keep my friends' needs on my mind,
so I can help them in many ways.

You have given me wonderful Christian
friends, Lord, who draw me closer to
You by challenging me to grow. This year,
help us to sharpen each other in faith.

Wherever I go, Lord, You have friends
for me, if I'm walking in Your will. Show
me those whom You want me to relate
closely to. Build my friendships,
no matter where I am.

As another year starts, bless each of
my friends, Jesus. May they cling to
You in faith and experience more
of Your love each day.

Some of my friends don't know You, Jesus.
Help me to love them well and share
the Good News You want each of them
to hear. I want to share eternity
with all those whom I love.

Give me wisdom, Lord, in choosing
new friends this year. They have a
powerful impact on my life, and I don't
want anyone leading me astray.

Friendship is such a blessing, Lord.
Over the next twelve months, may I treat
my friends as Your gifts to me, and may
I become a wonderful gift to them, too.

Jesus, when I'm with my friends,
am I talking or listening? Help me listen
more than I talk and ask concerned
questions about their lives.

Thank You, Lord, for giving me examples
of friendship in Your Word. When I need
to know what a real friend looks like,
I can see Your love for me and the love
of Your people for others. Make
my friendships those of faith.

Even though my friends haven't spoken about it, some of them are really hurting right now. Through Your Spirit, Lord, help me understand their pain and support them. If I can help, may they share their hurts with me.

Lord Jesus, can my friends rely on me for kindness, encouragement, and strength when they feel weak? Help me become a good friend who cares deeply for others and offers them Your truth in times of doubt.

I've given gifts to my friends, Lord, because they're special to me. But none of the earthly items I give are as important as Your Word. Help me share the gospel with all my friends who still don't love You.

I have a few good friends at work, Lord,
who never see much of my personal life
outside my career. Help me to be a whole
person who lives consistently whether
it's at work, home, or in the church.

I know disagreements can help or hurt my
friendships, Lord. Help me to see which
issues are important to work out and which
I need to bypass. I don't want bitterness
to intrude on my love for others.

Church friendships are some of the most
important ones I have, Lord. Help me
connect with my church friends outside
our services, and enable us to collaborate
on our greatest missions in life.

My Friends

MY FAMILY

No matter what family I'm part of,
it's the one You gave me, Lord.
Thank You for each member.
Help me cherish them all this year.

You have blessed me, Lord,
with a family who loves me.
Though I know they're not perfect,
neither am I. Help us support each other
through this year. Help me love
them well and wisely.

My Family

When I think of the ways You've
blessed both me and my family, Lord, I'm
completely humbled. Even members who
don't yet know You have been guided
by You in some ways. You've provided
for us all, in good times and lean
ones. Thank You, Jesus.

Lord, I have a physical family, but I also
have a spiritual one. I want to reach out
to my physical family so they will all
believe in You. But even if they never do,
You'll support me with Your own people.
Thank You for this double blessing.

Whether I've had great parents or disappointing ones, they're the ones You've given me. As I go forward in life, help me see Your purpose in choosing them just for me. I want to appreciate Your gift.

Thank You, Lord, for giving me my spouse to love deeply and romantically. We are both blessed by the love You've given us for each other. Help our love to reflect Your greater love and the commitment to You that we share.

Nothing surpasses Your love, O Lord,
but we see reflections of it in our family
lives. Help my family to shine Your
light on succeeding generations.

Thank You, Jesus, for my siblings.
With them I can share so many things
without needing to explain all the details.
They've known me so long and so well that
they can connect with me immediately.

Thank You, Lord, for my extended family.
Though we may not meet often, these
people are special to me. Bless them this
year, and help us to grow in love.

My children are a blessing, Lord, though
some days I don't see it. Help me to value
them daily, no matter what's happening
in my life. Don't let busyness
block out Your blessing.

Thank You for my spouse, Lord Jesus.
Together we can become an effective
team for You. Fill us daily with Your
Spirit as we seek to do Your will.

This year, when I get together
with my family, it can mean joy
or pain, Lord. No matter which,
help me love them for You.

My Family

The world often says awful things
about marriage, Lord. But it's Your gift that
joins people together. This year, help me
make my marriage a reflection of Your love.

In my spouse and me, You have
bonded two families together. May our
relationships with this larger family be
sweet and directed by Your Spirit. Help
us love one another as You commanded.

Love builds our home, Lord. Help me
remember that when challenges come my
way. I want to treat my family well this year
and help them draw closer to You because
of the life they've experienced here.

I love my family,
Lord. Help me to be a great blessing
to them for the next twelve months.
Keep me aware of their spiritual, physical,
and emotional needs. Help me to
help them grow in many ways.

Though I try to be a good parent, Lord,
I constantly learn of my own imperfections
in that area. Be my strength and wisdom
in the coming year so I can serve my
children and show them something of
what it's like to know You well.

My Family

Family relationships can teach me
so much about You, Lord. Through my
family You show me both Your love for
me and the love I need to give others.
Help me and my family be examples of
Your mercy and grace.

You tell me, Lord, that children are
a blessing. Sometimes it's easy to forget.
Help me develop close relationships with my
children—loving connections grounded in
faith in You and love for one another. Help
us all experience the blessings You offer.

My family needs security, Lord.
Help us develop it by basing our lives
on You and Your truths. You are truth,
and we can always trust in You.